Poppy Cotton is an ordinary girl
who lives in a pretty little cottage with
her mum and dad and the baby twins,
Angel and Archie. When she is good
everybody calls her Princess Poppy.
Her grandpa says that every
little girl is a princess, especially
when she is kind and helpful.
Are you kind and helpful too?

Honeypot Hill

*Can you find the places that
Poppy visits in this story?*

Saffron Thir
Sewing St

To the City

The Orchards

Lavender Valley
Garden Centre

Lavender Lake

Paddle Steamer
Quay

Healing House and Garden

The Worthingtons' House

Melody
Maker's Music
Shop

Lavender Lake
School of Dance

Bumble Bee's
Teashop

Peppermint
Pond

Hedgerows Hotel
where Mimosa lives

SCHOOL

Rosehip School

Summer Meadow

Christmas Corner

Wildspice Woods

*Visit Princess Poppy for fun, games,
puzzles, activities and lots more at*
www.princesspoppy.com

PUPPY LOVE
A RED FOX BOOK 978 0 552 57012 1

First published in Great Britain by Picture Corgi,
an imprint of Random House Children's Publishers UK
A Random House Group Company

This Red Fox edition published in 2013

1 3 5 7 9 10 8 6 4 2

Text copyright © Janey Louise Jones, 2010
Illustrations copyright © Picture Corgi Books, 2010
Illustrations by Veronica Vasylenko

The right of Janey Louise Jones and Veronica Vasylenko to be identified as the author and illustrator
of this work has been asserted in accordance with the Copyright, Designs and Patents Act 1988.

Red Fox Books are published by Random House Children's Publishers UK,
61–63 Uxbridge Road, London W5 5SA

www.**randomhousechildrens**.co.uk
www.**randomhouse**.co.uk
www.princesspoppy.com
Addresses for companies within The Random House Group Limited can be found at:
www.randomhouse.co.uk/offices.htm
THE RANDOM HOUSE GROUP Limited Reg. No. 954009
A CIP catalogue record for this book is available from the British Library.

Printed in China

Puppy Love

Written by Janey Louise Jones

RED FOX

For Buddy, a golden bundle of mischief.
And with thanks to Luella Wallace
who taught us puppy love.
★

Puppy Love

featuring

Mum
★

Dad
★

Princess Poppy

Honey
★

Mrs Meadowsweet
★

The puppies
★

"Hi, Poppy," called Honey as she walked up the garden path to Honeysuckle Cottage. "I'm so excited about seeing the puppies at Barley Farm!"

"Me too," replied Poppy. "Let's go!"

"This is going to be the best summer holiday ever!" said Poppy.

She loved puppies and had wanted one for ages. "We will be able to play with them every day!"

They found Mrs Meadowsweet in the cosy farmhouse kitchen.

Duchess, the sheepdog, was curled up with her ten new puppies.

"They are so sweet!" said the girls.

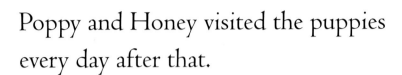

Poppy and Honey visited the puppies
every day after that.

Play time!

Nap time!

Tea time!

Fun in the farmyard!

My favourite!

First slipper!

Growing up so fast!

All ten puppies were cute but the smallest puppy was Poppy's favourite. Poppy named her Jasmine and secretly hoped that one day Jasmine would be hers.

"I wish I could have Jasmine," said Poppy as she and Honey walked home one afternoon.

"That would be amazing," replied Honey. "You should ask your parents."

"I know they will say no. They did when I asked if I could have a puppy before. They will say that a puppy is too much work," said Poppy glumly.

"But if you don't ask you will never know," answered Honey.

The next day Poppy and Honey went to Barley Farm as usual. Mrs Meadowsweet was making notices that said, 'PUPPIES FOR SALE'.

PUPPIES
FOR
SALE

"It is time for them to go to new families,"
she explained. "Will you help me write
the notices and put them up around
the village?"

Poppy hated the idea of Jasmine being
sold to another family, but she reluctantly
agreed to help.

When the notices were finished, the girls set off to put them up.

Poppy was very quiet.

"What is wrong?" asked Honey.

"I'm worried that another family is going to buy Jasmine and I will never see her again," said Poppy tearfully.

"Just ask your mum and dad if you can have her," replied Honey. "If you don't you will never know. You *have* to do it!"

Poppy waited until supper time.

"Mum, Dad," she said, "you know the puppies at Barley Farm? Mrs Meadowsweet is selling them and I wondered whether we could buy one."

Mum and Dad looked at one another.

"We *have* talked about getting a dog before," replied Mum. "I am sorry, darling, but the answer is no. You already have three pets, hardly any spare time, not to mention the expense and hard work involved in having a dog."

Poppy did not argue.

Posy

Flossy

MY HORSE

Twinkletoes

The next day, when Poppy and Honey
arrived at Barley Farm, the kitchen was
full of people holding the puppies.

When everyone finally left, Mrs Meadowsweet noticed that Poppy was looking sad. She asked her what the matter was.

"I asked if Mum and Dad would buy Jasmine but they said no," sobbed Poppy.

"You could take her for a trial day," suggested Mrs Meadowsweet. "That might change their minds!"

Poppy ran home and asked right away.

Mum and Dad went into the sitting room to talk about it. Poppy waited nervously in the kitchen.

"We have decided that one day can't hurt," said Dad when they came back.

"Bring her here tomorrow and we'll see," said Mum. "No promises though."

"Yippee!" replied Poppy. "I *know* you will love her."

Poppy and Honey went to collect the puppy early the next morning.

"Please be good, Jasmine!" Poppy whispered into the little pup's ear.

As soon as Poppy, Honey and Jasmine walked through the front door things started to go wrong.

Jasmine's waggy
tail knocked over
a vase,

she frightened Flossy the
cat with her barking,

chewed one of
Mum's slippers

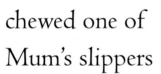

and she even started
digging up flowers in
the garden!

Just when Poppy thought things could not get any worse, Jasmine dashed back into the house and into Poppy's bedroom.

"Jasmine, come back, you naughty girl!" called Poppy.

"Oh, no!" said Honey when they caught up with her. "Look what she's done!"

Poppy came over to where Honey was and
noticed a little puddle on the floor.

"Quick, give me the tissues!" said Poppy.
"We need to clean this up. I'll never be
allowed to keep her if Mum and Dad
find out."

When Mrs Meadowsweet came to collect
Jasmine that afternoon, Poppy could hardly
bear to say goodbye. She was sure that
Mum and Dad would never agree to
keep the puppy now.

    She gave Jasmine
one last hug.

    Poppy felt sad. And she went to bed that
night feeling very sorry for herself.

But the next morning Poppy woke up with a start.

It was Jasmine jumping on her bed!

At first Poppy thought it was a dream, but she knew it was real when she saw Mum and Dad.

"Surprise!" they said.

"Wow!" gasped Poppy. "Can I really keep her?"

"As long as she stays away from slippers, vases and flowers, *and* you clean up all her little accidents!" laughed Dad.

"You have impressed us with the way you have looked after Jasmine," said Mum. "You are such a devoted little princess! And Jasmine *is* adorable. We couldn't let her go to another family!"

"Thank you!" smiled Poppy. She felt like the luckiest princess in the world.